The
RANCHO GORDO
POZOLE
Book

The RANCHO GORDO POZOLE Book

By STEVE SANDO

RANCHO GORDO PRESS

For the McKenzie Sisters,
Eileen Pharo and Maureen Crumly:
two women who have introduced me to
more good food and good times than anyone.

PHOTOGRAPHS **Steve Sando**

BOOK DESIGN **Meghan Hildebrand**

EDITOR **Julia Newberry**

COPYEDITOR **Anita Epler Crotty**

ISBN: 978-0-578-53305-6

Printed in China

10 9 8 7 6 5 4 3

RANCHO GORDO PRESS
1924 Yajome Street, Napa, CA 94559
www.ranchogordo.com

CONTENTS

ONE EVENING *in* GUADALAJARA

One warm night in the early 1980s, I found myself in the beautiful city of Guadalajara, in the Mexican state of Jalisco. A group of us were visiting local friends and taking in the best of the city — and, for a lot of people, that list of "bests" includes pozole, the fragrant hominy stew found in most regions of Mexico. In Jalisco, a chile-red, pork-rich version dominates, and our local hosts took us to their favorite *pozolería* to sample it.

Despite growing up in California, erroneously thinking I knew all there was to know about Mexico and Mexican food, I'd never tasted pozole... or even heard of it. The warm night, the beers, the new friends, the mariachis, and the intoxicating smells of delicious food hit me hard: I was in love. Following the example of the locals, I piled on the garnishes and added my dried oregano with a real flair. I took a sip of the soup — it was very spicy, but I was very macho and didn't blink when a bowl of chile de árbol salsa came my way. The Mexicans held their breath and cried, *"¡Se pica! ¡Cuidado!"* but I ignored them, somewhat to my regret. *!Ay, Chihuahua!* It was painfully hot.

At first, I couldn't taste anything but my tears. But as I calmed down, the flavors took over — and it was perfect. I was pale, and my eyes were bleary, but I was happy. I'd found my new favorite dish, a bowl that makes me cry and laugh at the same time. The blend — fresh garnishes and chewy, fluffy corn mingled in an excellent broth — was perfection. Raw radishes and lettuce balanced the slow-cooked meat. The lime juice lightened the dense, rich chile broth. Every aspect of this pozole was total heaven.

Years later, every bowl of pozole still sends me back to that Guadalajara evening of my youth. Even pozole variations from other parts of Mexico remind me of that night when I fell in love with the dish and its country.

If you're not a fan of spicy chiles, don't fret: I know quite a few Mexicans who don't care for the heat at all. There's magic in the dish without chiles, but I do hope you'll try a little heat, according to your own tastes.

If pozole is already a favorite dish of yours, I hope you'll find some tips and context in these pages. If you're new to the dish, I'm happy for you and flattered to be your guide.

I used to say that the secret to a great pozole was the broth. It's true that it's an essential element, but in

all honesty, all of the ingredients have to be excellent for this dish to work. Luckily, it's relatively simple; once you understand the components, you can master pozole and even improvise to make it your own.

There are a few twists and turns, but at its heart, pozole is no more than an elegant stew. At its most basic, pozole is a chile-infused soupy stew filled with hominy, and usually some kind of protein, which also helps make the broth. Hominy is corn that's had the skin removed — in this case, by cooking it in calcium hydroxide and then rubbing off the skins, a technique developed in Mesoamerica between 1,500 and 1,200 B.C.

To make pozole, cooked hominy is added to a broth — often the water used for cooking the pork that gives pozole its heartiness. Chiles can be part of the broth, or they can be added to a clear broth in the form of dry or fresh chiles or a chile-spiked salsa. Diners garnish the finished dish with fresh things like lettuce, avocados, and limes.

I've been cooking pozole for years. Although most recipes conform to the basic hominy-broth-chile blueprint, there's lots of room for discussion. Families and regions have their own way with pozole, and some of the recipes presented here are sure to offend someone's grandmother. (I apologize in advance.)

In addition to being a Mexican favorite, posole — in this case, spelled with an "s" — is also a traditional dish of the American southwest. My Mexican friends sometimes react strongly when they hear about the preparations up north, but I find it best to smile, shrug, and enjoy the marriage of corn, chiles, and broth in all its forms.

The recipes and ingredients may seem long and intimidating but you'll soon catch on to the rhythm of cooking pozole; I suspect my instructions will be more reference for you than a literal guide after you've made a few pots

—*Steve Sando*

POZOLE BASICS

MAKE
MINE
POZOLE

Pozole is one of the great iconic dishes of the world. I believe it to be on par with paella, cassoulet, *pho*, and chili con carne. It can be made modestly for a weeknight dinner, with enough leftovers for a terrific lunch. But it's really a showstopper, designed to be enjoyed with a crew of people you love. For some of us, the mere idea of pozole puts us in a good mood.

Corn, chiles, and pork are not such an unusual combination in the Mexican kitchen. Something about this soupy stew is almost universally appreciated. California chef Pilar Sanchez adds many nontraditional seasonal fresh vegetables like zucchini, carrots, and chayote to her version. Despite being rather unorthodox, it would be very hard not to like it. At the celebrated Mexico City restaurant Pujol, I enjoyed a deconstructed pozole from chef Enrique Olvera — clever and beautiful, but clearly pozole.

In researching pozole, I was happy to discover that almost no one likes canned hominy, but sad to find that most people use it anyway. Pork seems to reign supreme as pozole protein, but some cooks prefer chicken — especially those who feel pork is greasy.

Pozole as a celebration meal has roots in Mesoamerica. The stew — known as *pozolli* in the Nahuatl language — was eaten by the Mexica people as a kind of Communion on feast days, and it included meat from conquered warriors. The protein choice wasn't a culinary preference; it was a ceremonial tribute to the god Xipe Totéc. The Mexica (who you may have known as Aztecs in your school days) felt that food was life, and consuming life begets stronger life. *Pozolli* was a very serious dish, according to Bernardino de Sahagún, a 16th century Franciscan Catholic priest who documented a great deal of indigenous life and is considered the first New World anthropologist.

Moving ahead to modern times, pozole has shed its cannibalistic origins. It's often served alongside tostadas and sour cream but, in general, it's a one-pot wonder and a great party dish. The instructions might seem daunting but remember: this is all the work you have to do for your entire feast, unless you want dessert. (A good flan is always welcome.) For this meal, you can forget about multiple courses, side dishes, and salads. The whole fiesta is in the bowl.

CORN

In order for corn to transform into a pozole-worthy ingredient, it requires some special treatment. The process, known as nixtamalization, takes dried field corn and makes it both palatable and digestible. If you were to cook unprocessed dried corn, even for days, not much would happen; it needs to be treated to become tasty.

When corn arrived from the Americas, northern Italians embraced it as a staple, grinding it into cornmeal to make porridge. Everyone loves polenta; it's delicious and filling. But using it as a main source of nutrition and sustenance led many Italians to suffer from pellagra, a debilitating disease caused by a lack of niacin. (I'll spare you a description of the gruesome symptoms.)

In contrast, the early Mexicans consumed much more corn than the Italians but never suffered the same fate, because they had mastered the art of nixtamalization — cooking dried kernels with calcium hydroxide — to release niacin and help make the grain more digestible by humans. Beans and chiles helped the ancient societies of Mexico build their empire, but it was nixtamalized corn that fueled the construction of the pyramids and the development of an advanced society.

To make hominy — another name for nixtamalized corn — dried corn kernels are cooked in a mixture of water and *cal* — short for calcium hydroxide, also known as powdered limestone or lime — and then left to soak. (The "lime" used in nixtamalization is a food-grade version of the soil amendment you add to your garden, not the citrus fruit.) After soaking, the corn is rinsed, and its skin — technically known as the pericarp — falls away with a minimum amount of rubbing. The treated corn is known as nixtamal. You can grind it to make masa for tortillas, or it's ready to use in pozole.

At the base of each kernel of corn is a small nib known as the tip cap, where the kernel attached itself to the cob. After nixtamalization, the tip cap becomes a piece of flavorless fiber. In Mexico, it's expected that you pinch off the tip cap and discard it, or give it to your chickens. Leaving the nib won't really affect the flavor of the pozole — and really, it's nice to have some extra fiber — but if you remove it, the kernel will blossom beautifully during its long simmer. As part of the Mexica peoples' ritual consumption of *pozolli*, the "white flower" of the opened kernel was symbolic and very much a part of the rite. The tradition lingers today: I've been to a *pozolería* in Mexico with my Mexican friends who were put off by the vendor who left the nib, despite the fact that her pozole was delicious.

Nixtamalization is obviously a lot of work for anyone, especially for a casual home cook. In the United States, some Mexican markets sell nixtamal in the refrigerated section — and of course, there are the ubiquitous cans of hominy. The cans are okay in a pinch, but, for me, they're a compromise. Real nixtamal, simmering away on the stove, smells like having a large, wet tortilla in your kitchen. There's nothing quite like it.

This all leads me to prepared hominy, a product of the American southwest. Fresh corn is dried by commercial processors, and then producers nixtamalize it, cook it just enough to remove the skin, then dry it again. When you get the hominy home, you simply simmer it in water — perhaps with some onions — and, in about an hour and a half, it's cooked and ready to use. Normally it blossoms like traditional nixtamal, only the "flower" is on the other end of the kernel: The tip cap remains — lending the final product some extra fiber — and the other end is diffused from all the cooking.

Prepared hominy is what we sell at Rancho Gordo; our version is made using a smaller kernel than what you'd find in typical Mexican corn, although we occasionally make it with larger kernels or colored kernels. The indigenous cultures of the American southwest call both the grain and the final dish posole (with an "s"), and you can find it made with red or blue corn in addition to the white or yellow kernels you'd find in Mexico. I've even seen mixtures of white, red, and blue kernels — they look pretty in their packages but, once cooked, the final effect is somewhat murky and unappetizing. The red varieties tend to have less natural fat, so they taste a little "healthy" to most people, but it's worth a try if you get a chance.

Many Mexicans will tell you the preferred corn variety for pozole is an old heirloom variety of white dent maize called *cacahuacintle* (or *cacahuazintle*). It's used almost exclusively for making pozole, and it's a safe bet, but there are other varieties worth exploring, especially some of the heirloom varieties.

"*Cacahuacintle* is just one of many pozole corns," says Rafael Meier, my friend in Mexico City, "but it is not necessarily the preferred one. We have many different corns that are actually used in pozole. It all depends on the climate and culture of the region."

Rafael, who is working to preserve the heritage grains of Mexico through his group, Fundación Tortilla de Maíz Mexicana, says that in the states of Morelos and Guerrero, the heirloom corn of choice for pozole would be *ancho*, which means wide. In Nayarit, the corn would be *jala*. Oaxacans prefer *bolita*, while in Jalisco and Michoacán, the preferred corn would be a group known as *elotes occidentales*.

"*Cacahuacintle* has become renowned because it is the corn that is grown near Mexico City," says Rafael. "But states like Jalisco and Guerrero, which are famous for pozole, don't use *cacahuacintle*."

Fair warning for traveling cooks: In Mexico, the word pozole only refers to the final dish. If you were to ask for pozole in a Mexican market, they would think you were asking for a bowl of soup. If you want the grain, ask for *maiz pozolero* — and understand that you'd need to process it with *cal* to make nixtamal (see Making Nixtamal from Dried Corn, below). I've never seen prepared hominy in Mexico, or even met a Mexican who isn't confused by the idea of it at first. But most of the Mexican home cooks on staff at Rancho Gordo who take home the prepared hominy agree it's far superior to the canned stuff.

Making Nixtamal from Dried Corn

Boil 6 quarts of water in a large stockpot; add 2 to 2.5 pounds of dried corn. Once the water reaches a full boil, add an ounce of calcium hydroxide to the pot. Within seconds, the corn will turn a lurid yellow. Lower the heat; simmer for 10 minutes. Turn off the heat and allow the mixture to rest at least 6 hours, or overnight.

After resting, the skins will separate from the corn, and the water will be a little murky. Drain the corn, reserving the liquid for your garden or houseplants.

Under running water, rub the corn to remove the skins.

From each kernel, pinch off the tip cap — the small nib where the kernel attached itself to the cob — and discard.

Return the nixtamal to the pot; add water to cover by 2 inches. Add some crushed garlic cloves, onion slices, and a bay leaf. Bring to a simmer and cook until done: The kernels will blossom but they should have some tooth to them. At this point, they are cooked and ready to be used in any recipe calling for cooked nixtamal or hominy.

COOKING PREPARED HOMINY

Of all the ways to cook dried hominy, simmering in a trusty soup pot on the stove is the most reliable. Basically, you just soak and simmer.

The first thing you must do is to check that, in fact, you have hominy. After trying a recipe from my blog, one writer — who, I want to stress, was using a non-Rancho Gordo product — was very upset. "Heirloom pazole [sic] needs to cook at least 4 or 5 hours, even after it has been soaked for 5 hours. It is totally raw after just two hours of hard cooking." The writer was using dried, untreated corn. Because it wasn't nixtamalized, it would never be pleasant, no matter how long they had cooked it.

You can — and should — use the cooked hominy right away; hominy is best when freshly prepared. If you end up having more than you immediately need, you can refrigerate cooked hominy for a few days, or freeze it in some of its cooking liquid for up to two months.

Make sure you allow enough time to soak the prepared hominy for 5 to 8 hours. It won't swell up in the same way dried beans do, but it will be doing its work.

FOR COOKED POSOLE:

½ pound Rancho Gordo Prepared
Hominy/White Corn Posole

½ of an onion, chopped

A half-pound of dried hominy — about 1 cup —
yields approximately 4 cups of cooked hominy.

ON THE STOVETOP:

In a large bowl, soak prepared hominy in enough
water to cover by 2 inches; let sit 5 to 8 hours.

In a large stockpot over high heat, combine
the prepared hominy and its soaking water.
Add additional water, if needed, to cover the
hominy by about 2 inches. Add the onion; bring
to a boil. Cook for 10 minutes, then reduce
heat to medium-low. Continue cooking at a
gentle simmer until the prepared hominy is
tender, about 90 minutes. Partially cover the
pot as needed to regulate heat, but don't cover
completely or hominy may turn gummy.

Check occasionally, adding hot water from a
kettle, as needed, to keep the corn covered by
about an inch. The hominy is done when it's
no longer chalky but retains some texture. The
kernel will also pop at one end, causing the
hominy to blossom. (Because life is unfair, once
in awhile you will get a batch that won't flower.)

Strain the hominy, reserving at least 2 cups of the
cooking liquid for use in your pozole. Refrigerate
or freeze any additional liquid for another use.

IN THE PRESSURE COOKER:

Pressure cooking can be fast and efficient, but
my experiments have shown that it's not an ideal
way to cook prepared hominy. Cooking the corn
for 20 to 40 minutes after soaking, followed by
a natural release, yields cooked hominy with a
gummy, unappealing texture and mediocre broth.
I've had people tell me that they've successfully
made pozole in an electric pressure cooker or
Instant Pot, but I haven't been able to replicate
satisfactory results. I've had some victories
making beans in a pressure cooker, but success
with hominy has eluded me. It might be worth
experimenting if you're an enthusiast — drop us a
line and let us know how you fare.

IN THE SLOW COOKER:

A long 6-to 10-hour soak followed by about
5 hours in a modern slow cooker set to high heat
will yield fine results, but it doesn't seem all
that much more convenient than the stovetop
method. After the corn has been cooked, take
the lid off and let the whole thing breathe a bit
before using in your pozole.

It's important to note that slow cookers vary
widely and some cook cooler or hotter than
others. You'll need to experiment to find your
sweet spot.

MEAT AND POULTRY

There are many competing opinions about the best meat for pozole, but no matter where you stand on this debate, be aware that in Mexico, pork rules. Except when it doesn't. I've made a lot of chicken pozole in my day, but when I mentioned this to a Mexican friend, she laughed. "Why would you go to all the trouble of making pozole and then just have chicken. In Mexico, it's almost always pork!"

I ran this by some friends from Michoacán and in their family, chicken in pozole rojo was the standard. Another friend from Nayarit confessed that his mother made the best pozole and she used both pork and chicken, except when they were having a shrimp pozole. History tells us that armadillo and turkey were even used. In some parts of Mexico, like on the Costa Chica of Guerrero and Oaxaca, they like tins of sardines. I will try this one day, but there seem to be so many other delicious options to explore first.

When cooking for a big crowd — and pozole is the perfect dish to feed the masses — a whole or half pig's head is the standard. In their book, *In the Charcuterie,* Toponia Miller and Taylor Boetticher note that pig's head offers the perfect blend of meat, bone, cartilage, and skin to make a rich dish. Taylor and Toponia put the head in a big pot with enough cold water to cover it all, then set it on the stove for a 3-hour simmer with bay leaves and oregano. Once cooked, the strained broth is where they cook the rest of the pork (they like pork shoulder). It's delicious and will make a crowd happy.

For smaller crowds, a head isn't always practical — I tend to serve 6 to 8 people, sometimes up to 10, so even a half-head isn't ideal. According to my own experimentation and conversations with other pozole aficionados, smaller batches can use a combination of a bone-in pork shoulder, a trotter, and bone-in country-style ribs to great effect. Many Mexican recipes call for *espinazo* — literally, spine — though the closest analog in the States is what we call country-style pork ribs: meat from the blade near the shoulder. A pig trotter, chopped into six pieces (either by your butcher or with a big cleaver and mallet) adds flavor and a rich texture that muscle-meat alone can't supply.

Pork shoulder is easy enough to get; more and more, country-style ribs are widely available. For the trotters, and especially the head, you'll want to order ahead from your butcher. I buy three trotters at a time, using one for a batch of pozole, and stashing two bags with the rest in the freezer for the next round.

For a large pot of pozole, using ½ pound of cooked prepared hominy (around 4 cups) and 2 to 4 pounds of mixed pork makes a good amount of meat. Don't get too caught up in the exact quantities of each specific type of meat, but remember that a mix will produce a better-tasting broth. Fat, skin, and bones play important roles alongside the meat.

If you're using chicken, it makes most sense to cut up a whole bird and to remove the pieces as they finish cooking — especially the temperamental breasts, which can turn rubbery or dry at a moment's notice. Bone-in thighs work fine if you want to stick to pieces instead. Using chicken breasts alone would yield a bland broth — and again, there's the danger of overcooking; thighs and legs are much more forgiving. When my butcher has chicken feet, I buy a bag and separate them into batch-size freezer bags so I always have some handy. They are a little disturbing to look at but, like pig trotters, they add an unbeatable depth and viscosity to the broth.

A PLEA FOR QUALITY MEAT

Recently I made a French daube with meat from a gourmet butcher. I was using braising cuts and was shocked by the high price. I smiled and made a mental note never to do that again. The daube was fabulous — so fabulous that I decided to make it a week later, this time getting the exact same cuts from the grocery store and following the same recipe. The entire family agreed without prompting that the version I'd made with sustainably raised, grass-fed beef was dramatically superior. For all my hard work, using cheap meat was no bargain. For your pozole, heritage pork is more than a fad, and well worth looking for. The same goes with well-cared-for, pastured chickens.

If possible, befriend your butcher and seek their advice. They know what they're talking about, and — even though the prices tend to be higher than the supermarket — they can help you save money by suggesting more reasonably priced cuts.

CHILES

In the American southwest, it's common to use chile powder to season and flavor posole. This method is incredibly simple but you must make sure the powder is thoroughly cooked or you'll end up with a grainy texture. If you go this route, try sautéing onions and garlic in oil or lard, then adding your chile powder and frying the paste. To make the sauce, you slowly add broth or water to the well-cooked paste.

In Mexico, it's more traditional to quickly toast whole chiles before rehydrating them in warm water. The chiles are blended and then added to the soup. It sounds like it might be a lot of bother but, once you get the habit, it's delicious and you won't think twice about the process. To make a chile sauce, heat some lard or oil, then fry the pureed chile mixture in the pan. This method isn't universal for pozole, but it's a common Mexican way to make a chile sauce.

Choosing which chiles to use is a personal (and regional) decision, but you'll be safe if you use a ratio of half ancho chiles and half guajillo chiles, perhaps erring on the side of a few extra guajillos. The anchos, which are dried poblano chiles, provide body and substance, while guajillos give untamed, fruity fire to the dish. I've had some very mild (and disappointing) guajillos, so you'll need to test for their zing factor.

Most chiles need to be soaked in warm water before blending. The easiest method is to warm a pan of water on the stove while you toast the chiles. By the time you're done toasting, the water will be warm. Using hot tap water isn't a good idea — the water has been sitting in your water heater for goodness knows how long, and studies have confirmed that this isn't a good way to cook. Start with cold water, fresh from the tap.

As far as chile toasting goes, remember it should be a gentle, brief process — if you're not careful, you can burn your chiles and give them a bitter flavor. On a hot skillet or comal (the traditional Mexican griddle), gently flatten the chiles with a spatula, then release. The smell should be nutty and rich, and you may see the slightest wisp of steam rise off of the chiles. Flip them over, toast the other side, then drop the chiles into the waiting pan of warm water. That's it.

If you have a hard time regulating heat on your stove, it's better not to toast them at all than to use burnt chiles. Once in a blue moon, despite your best efforts, you may get a bitter chile mix, even without overtoasting. Sometimes adding the smallest amount of sugar to the resulting sauce can help overcome the bitter taste.

Most Mexican cooks serve pozole with a painfully spicy chile de árbol salsa or a bowl of chile powder, often made from outrageously hot pequín peppers. Pozole blanco often comes with a relish (see page 124) of pickled onions and habanero chiles — a mixture that tastes great on a lot of dishes, especially quesadillas.

BROTH

You'll be making your own broth by poaching meat and reserving the liquid. Many cuts of pork and chicken are very fatty and (while no one around here is judging you for your love of fat) it'll make your pozole more pleasant if you de-fat the broth.

Once the meat is cooked, allow it to cool a bit. Separate the meat from the bones and skin; when it's cool enough to handle, shred it into more manageable pieces. Remember, pozole is served with just a spoon! Everything in the bowl should be bite-size.

Once the broth has cooled close to room temperature, it goes in the refrigerator until it's well chilled. The fat will rise to the top of the bowl — sometimes it's a shocking amount, depending on what cuts of meat you've used. Gently remove the fat; if there's a lot, you may be able to lift the disc right off the broth, but otherwise use a strainer or a slotted

spoon. Be sure to save the removed fat for another use. It's infused with all of the meaty, seasoned flavors, and will add depth to anything you cook in it.

If you're in a hurry, you can use a fat separator, a special measuring cup with a spout at the base. You ladle in the broth, and the fat rises, leaving the broth at the bottom near the spout. But honestly, your best tool is time. Make your broth early — even a day or two ahead — and then you just don't have to worry about it. Once the broth is de-fatted, it's ready to be reheated and used in your pozole.

If you're making vegetarian pozole, things aren't quite so easy. Often in Mexico, cooks use chicken broth for a delicious pozole without actual meat in the bowl, but I know most vegetarians wouldn't consider this acceptable. You can use commercial vegetable broth, but it's better to make your own. Generally, vegetable broths don't need more than an hour of gentle simmering to prepare.

Simmer an onion, some garlic, and vegetable trimmings in water to make a rich liquid. When I'm ambitious, I save these scraps and freeze them until I have enough; corn cobs and corn silk are especially delicious broth ingredients.

For fish and seafood broths, 40 minutes simmering bones and heads is about standard. If you're making shrimp — either for pozole or any other recipe — buy raw, shell-on shrimp, fresh or frozen, and use the shells to make a quick, dreamy broth with onions, celery, garlic, and Mexican oregano. I also add about a tablespoon of Asian fish sauce, a secret ingredient that is not at all traditional. It's surprisingly cuisine-neutral and, for me, makes more culinary sense than the more common Mexican shrimp powder, which can get murky if overused.

If you're making a seafood or fish pozole and don't have shells or bones, it's fine to use chicken broth.

GARNISHES

Alongside steaming hot bowls of pozole, you'll want to lay out a table full of garnishes and condiments: This is really what makes pozole a party food. Guests pass around the bowls, doctoring their pozole to their own tastes — in reality, most people want a little bit of everything.

As a host, this is a great chance to show your thoughtfulness and generosity. A huge bowl piled with thinly sliced lettuce or cabbage costs pennies but feels generous and abundant. The same goes for radishes, onions, and the other parts of the dish. Don't scrimp! You can make a salad tomorrow with the leftovers. A table brimming with bowls of garnishes surrounding a big pot of steaming soup, waiting to be served, is a vision your guests will always remember.

LETTUCE VERSUS CABBAGE

There's an old saying about Mexican quirkiness: "They put the salad in the soup!" Most garnish spreads will feature plenty of finely cut lettuce to pile on to your pozole. I've had it many times with cabbage, also thinly sliced, but fans of lettuce think the cabbage idea is truly bizarre. You should do what you like but be prepared for some opinions should you serve cabbage to someone from central Mexico. I personally prefer cabbage with a rich, fatty soup: it doesn't wilt, it's a nice contrast to the pozole, and I miss the crunch when I'm served lettuce. But lettuce seems to be the standard. One Mexican chef told me he likes to use baby heirloom lettuce.

It's partly a matter of taste and it's partly regional. If you are using lettuce, ignore the chef who uses baby lettuce and make sure it's super crisp. Don't cut it until right before serving, to keep it at its best. My preference would be romaine lettuce, but iceberg is not uncommon. Personally, I pile it on.

RADISHES

Radishes are a key pozole garnish. Their crunch is a wonderful contrast to the rich broth and keeps things fresh.

You can cut them thin with a mandoline or practice your knife skills. They should be fresh, raw, red, and sitting in a bowl of ice water. In Oaxaca, I've seen cooks add a little salt to the water, which gives them a delicious buttery taste.

CHILE POWDER AND CHILE SAUCES

A bowl of chile powder — often ground pequín peppers — is normally available for the diners who crave more heat in their pozole. Other times, you'll find a fiery salsa made from chiles de árbol. This sauce tends to be very simple and not always terribly interesting on its own — but with the rich broth, it's a natural.

It's important to check that your chiles come from Mexico or the United States. Unfortunately, Chinese chiles, especially chiles de árbol, have flooded the market and they tend to be very harsh and metallic tasting. Good chiles de árbol should be searingly hot, but they also bring a nutty flavor. You should be smiling through your tears of pain.

Another chile garnish — typically served with pozole blanco — is a simple relish of habanero chiles and white onions, sliced super thin, resting in vinegar or lime juice. If you find the pickled chiles too hot for your taste, you can eat just the onions, which will have soaked up some of the chiles' heat and flavor from the brine. Try this pickle with manzano chiles (also known as peron or canario) if you can find them. This regional option lacks the punch of a habanero but brings meatier flesh and a nice, tropical flavor.

CILANTRO

I always assumed that cilantro was one of the traditional garnishes for pozole, but Mexican cooks have assured me that it is not. So you've been warned! Cilantro is a key *ingredient* in pozole verde, but only as part of the sauce, not as a garnish to pass around the table. Recipes that include cilantro as one of the garnishes tend not to be written by Mexican cooks. They may hail from New Mexico and other parts of the U.S., but not *Madre México*. If you love it and want to serve it, by all means, add it to your table — just know that it might confuse a Mexican friend. (I'm sure they have a long list of your quirks already and this would be one of the very minor issues.)

50 The Rancho Gordo Pozole Book

DRIED OREGANO

There are many types of Mexican oregano and none of them are true oregano species, the kind we know from Europe. The most common Mexican oregano is *Lippia graveolens*. It's similar to oregano but it's milder and has a more citrusy flavor. As part of our Rancho Gordo-Xoxoc Project, we're working with a cooperative in the Huasteca region of Hidalgo to import their local oregano, which we market as Oregano Indio. This variety is *Poliomintha longiflora A. Gray* and the hints of citrus are replaced with an earthy floral flavor.

A sense of drama is essential as you add your oregano to your bowl of hot pozole. Take a good-size pinch in your palms and then raise your arms above the bowl and rub the oregano into the pozole, letting it cascade into the waiting broth. Trust me, it's a lot of fun and it makes your pozole taste terrific.

MINCED ONIONS

A bowl of finely chopped white onions is also an essential part of the pozole table. Except in the Yucatan, where red onions are predominant, onions in Mexico tend to be white. If you serve nothing else, you want onions and limes as garnish.

Yellow onions are more common in the U.S., but they are juicier and more pungent than white onions. If you only have yellow onions on hand, you can rinse them in cold water after chopping, then drain them to remove some of their bite.

LIMES

Acid is crucial when creating a balanced bowl of pozole. Mexican limes — what we know as key limes in the U.S. — are small, juicy, and have just the right amount of acid. Persian limes — the large ones sold in most grocery stores —are fine but expensive, bolder, and a little harder to squeeze. To my taste, key limes are a little bit sweeter.

Cut the limes into quarters and pile in a small bowl. And no, you cannot substitute lemons for limes. The seeds in both varieties are unpleasant but lime seeds are not intensely bitter like lemon seeds.

TOSTADAS AND SOUR CREAM

It may seem odd to eat a big bowl of corn soup with more corn, but tostadas — fried corn tortillas — are almost always served on the side, sometimes even spread with sour cream. I will confess that it strikes me as odd, much the same as the American practice of serving garlic bread alongside spaghetti: wheat with more wheat. Is it too much of a good thing? I'll leave that up to you. I offer tostadas to guests, but rarely eat them myself.

Regarding the cream, I have heard of families that add sour cream and even cheese to the pozole itself. I just can't. To me, a bowl of good pozole is perfection and adding dairy seems weird.

CHILE de ÁRBOL SALSA

Chiles de árbol are short, pointy little bullets of pain and joy. They are most commonly used in simple table salsas. When toasted very briefly, they have a nutty flavor. I've had them deep-fried and added to a meat taco and they were delicious, but they were challenging to my otherwise iron constitution.

These sauces may seem simple and possibly even boring, but keep in mind that their role is to complement the pozole, not be the main event.

Make sure your chiles were grown in Mexico or California, or use a brand or farmer that you trust.

CHILE de ÁRBOL SALSA NUMBER ONE

1 cup dried chiles de árbol, wiped clean with a moist towel, stems removed

½ cup pineapple vinegar or apple cider vinegar

Juice of 4 Mexican limes or key limes

1 teaspoon ground cumin

2 garlic cloves, peeled

Salt, to taste

Warm a dry comal or skillet over medium heat; toast the chiles quickly, taking care not to let them burn.

In a bowl, combine the toasted chiles, vinegar, and lime juice; let the chiles hydrate for 15 minutes.

In a blender, process the chiles, cumin, and garlic until smooth. Blend well, scraping down the paste as needed. Use a wooden spoon to push the mixture through a fine-mesh sieve into a small bowl, discarding the skins and seeds. Taste and add salt, as desired.

CHILE de ÁRBOL SALSA NUMBER TWO

½ cup dried chiles de árbol, wiped clean with a moist towel, stems removed

1 clove garlic, peeled

Salt

In a small saucepan, warm 2 cups of water over medium-low heat; turn off heat when the water is hot.

Meanwhile, warm a dry comal or skillet over medium heat; toast the chiles quickly, taking care not to let the chiles burn.

Soak the toasted chiles in the pan of warm water for 15 minutes. Drain chiles, reserving the soaking liquid.

In a blender, combine the chiles, garlic, and a pinch of salt, plus enough of the strained chile-soaking liquid to allow the blender blades to move. Blend well, scraping down the paste as needed.

RED

CLASSIC PORK POZOLE

This is the classic pozole of central Mexico. You might find some regional or personal variances to the cuts of pork or the combination of chiles, but if I were bold enough to serve this to a Mexican grandmother (spoiler: I'm not) I'm confident that she would recognize this recipe as pozole. And personally, I would happily eat this dish anytime.

Some families fry the chiles, as I've done; others just add the blended chile mixture to the broth. If you are lax about de-fatting your pork broth, avoid frying the chile paste or you'll end up with a very greasy soup.

If you can get a pig's head — or even half of one — it's worth the effort. Not to be preachy, but if we're going to eat meat, it's important to not waste any part of the animal, even when it seems strange or gives us pause. The head has more meat than you'd think, but not enough to cover the whole recipe, so you'll still need to supplement with pork shoulder.

CLASSIC PORK POZOLE *serves 8 to 12*

FOR THE MEAT AND BROTH:

2 to 4 pounds bone-in pork shoulder, chopped into large chunks

1 pound bone-in country-style pork ribs

1 pig trotter (optional), chopped into 6 pieces

½ of a white or yellow onion, peeled and sliced

3 garlic cloves, peeled and smashed

1 tablespoon salt, or to taste

2 bay leaves

3 black peppercorns, roughly cracked

FOR THE CHILE PASTE:

2 ancho chiles, wiped clean with a moist towel

3 guajillo chiles, wiped clean with a moist towel

½ of an onion, chopped

6 garlic cloves, peeled and smashed

2 tablespoons oil or lard

TO FINISH:

4 to 6 cups cooked prepared hominy, plus 2 cups of reserved cooking liquid (see page 30)

GARNISHES:

Radishes, sliced thin

Onion, finely chopped

Chile de Árbol Salsa (see page 56)

Dried Mexican oregano or
Rancho Gordo Oregano Indio

Romaine or iceberg lettuce, sliced very thin

Mexican limes or key limes, quartered

Avocado, cubed

Corn tostadas and sour cream

FOR THE MEAT AND BROTH:

In a large stockpot over medium-high heat, add the pork shoulder, ribs, trotter, onion, garlic, salt, bay leaves, peppercorns, and enough water to cover meat by 1 inch. Bring to a boil, then immediately reduce heat to a gentle simmer, using a lid to help regulate temperature as needed. Skim and discard any impurities that rise to the top. Continue to simmer for several hours, until meat is tender and falling off the bones.

Remove the pork pieces to a platter. Once cool enough to handle, separate the meat, discarding bones and skin. Strain the broth into a very large bowl; cool to room temperature. Chill in the refrigerator for several hours, or overnight, until fat rises to the top of the bowl and congeals. Remove the fat and reserve for another use.

FOR THE CHILE PASTE:

Cut chiles in half; discard seeds and stems. In a small saucepan, warm 2 cups of water over medium-low heat; turn off heat when the water is hot. Meanwhile, warm a dry comal or skillet over medium heat; toast the chiles quickly, taking care not to let the chiles burn. Soak the toasted chiles in the pan of warm water for 15 minutes.

In a blender, combine the chiles, onion, garlic, and enough of the strained chile-soaking liquid to allow the blender blades to move. Blend well, scraping down the paste as needed. Use a wooden spoon to push the mixture through a wide-mesh sieve into a bowl, discarding skins and seeds.

In a large pot over medium heat, warm the oil until hot, 2 to 3 minutes. Add the chile paste and stir immediately. Reduce heat to medium-low; cook, stirring frequently, for 5 to 10 minutes. Taste and adjust seasoning, as desired.

TO FINISH:

To the pot with the chile paste, add the reserved pork meat and the drained cooked hominy. (If you are using canned hominy, rinse the kernels before using and discard the liquid.) You can break up large pieces of meat as needed, but generally they'll do this on their own.

Slowly add about 6 cups of the broth, enough to make a soupy stew, stirring constantly. If the pozole is not soupy enough to your liking, slowly add the reserved hominy-cooking liquid (or tap water, if you used canned hominy) or more broth, until you reach the desired consistency.

Continue cooking, stirring occasionally, until all of the ingredients are warmed through, about 20 minutes (or longer if you've pulled your pork and corn from the refrigerator).

Ladle into bowls and serve with your preferred garnishes.

VARIATIONS

The late, great chef Patricia Quintana's recipe for Jalisco-style pozole includes both pork and chicken, as many do. She also added a stale bolillo roll soaked in vinegar, squeezed to remove the excess liquid, then added to the blender with the chiles.

Chef Gonzalo Guzmán of San Francisco's Nopalito restaurant makes his pozole from pure pork shoulder but purees a cup of the hominy with a cup of broth before adding it back to the final pozole. He uses all ancho chiles instead of a mix, and prefers cabbage to lettuce for his garnish.

RED
CHICKEN POZOLE

When cooking chicken pozole, it's best to use dark meat, as breasts can overcook in an instant. If you insist on using white meat, be sure to time the cooking and remove it after 25 minutes of gentle poaching. Legs and thighs are much more forgiving and, if you go over the suggested cooking times, it's not generally a problem.

You easily can cut a whole chicken into parts. I really like using chicken feet in the broth, and I save chicken backs in my freezer for just this kind of dish. There are no hard rules here.

I know of cooks who cook the whole dish in one pot but I think it's hard to de-fat the broth, and the flavors can get muddy. Preparing the different components, mostly a day ahead, and then marrying them right before serving time keeps the flavors more distinct.

RED CHICKEN POZOLE

serves 8 to 12

FOR THE MEAT AND BROTH:

4 skin-on chicken thighs

4 skin-on chicken drumsticks

1 chicken back

2 chicken feet, chopped

½ of an onion, sliced

3 garlic cloves, peeled and smashed

2 bay leaves

3 black peppercorns, roughly cracked

1 tablespoon salt, or to taste

FOR THE CHILE PASTE:

2 ancho chiles, wiped clean with a moist towel

3 guajillo chiles, wiped clean with a moist towel

½ of an onion, chopped

6 garlic cloves, smashed and peeled

2 tablespoons oil or lard

TO FINISH:

4 to 6 cups cooked prepared hominy, plus 2 cups of reserved cooking liquid (see page 30)

GARNISHES:

Radishes, sliced thin

Onion, finely chopped

Chile de Árbol Salsa (see page 56)

Dried Mexican oregano or
Rancho Gordo Oregano Indio

Romaine or iceberg lettuce, sliced very thin

Mexican limes or key limes, quartered

Avocado, cubed

Tostadas (optional)

FOR THE MEAT AND BROTH
(BEST DONE A DAY AHEAD):

In a large stockpot over high heat, combine the chicken thighs, drumsticks, back, and feet; onion, garlic, bay leaves, peppercorns, salt, and 8 cups of water. Bring to a boil, then immediately reduce heat to a gentle simmer, using a lid to help regulate temperature as needed. Cook until the chicken is done, about an hour. If you're substituting chicken breasts, remove them after 25 to 30 minutes so they don't overcook.

Remove pan from heat. Remove the chicken pieces to a platter. Once cool enough to handle, separate the meat, discarding bones and skin.

Strain the broth into a very large bowl; cool to room temperature. Chill in the refrigerator for several hours, or overnight, until fat rises to the top of the bowl and congeals. Remove the fat and reserve for another use.

FOR THE CHILE PASTE:

Cut chiles in half; discard seeds and stems. In a small saucepan, warm 2 cups of water over medium-low heat; turn off heat when the water is hot. Meanwhile, warm a dry comal or skillet over medium heat; toast the chiles quickly, taking care not to let the chiles burn. Soak the toasted chiles in the pan of warm water for 15 minutes. Drain chiles, reserving the soaking liquid.

In a blender, combine the chiles, onion, garlic, and enough of the strained chile-soaking liquid to allow the blender blades to move. Blend well, scraping down the paste as needed. Use a wooden spoon to push the mixture through a fine-mesh sieve into a bowl, discarding skins and seeds.

In a large pot over medium heat, warm the oil until hot, 2 to 3 minutes. Add the chile paste and stir immediately. Reduce heat to medium-low; cook, stirring frequently, for 5 to 10 minutes. Taste and adjust seasoning, as desired.

TO FINISH:

To the pot with the chile paste, add the reserved meat and the drained cooked hominy. (If you are using canned hominy, rinse the kernels before using and discard the liquid.)

Slowly add about 6 cups of broth, enough to make a soupy stew, stirring constantly. If the pozole is not soupy enough to your liking, slowly add the reserved hominy-cooking liquid (or tap water, if you used canned hominy) or more broth, until you reach the desired consistency.

Continue cooking over medium heat, stirring occasionally, until all of the ingredients are warmed through, about 20 minutes (or a bit longer if you've pulled your chicken and corn from the refrigerator).

Ladle into bowls and serve with your preferred garnishes.

SOUTHWESTERN RED PORK POSOLE

The real difference between this pork dish and a more traditional Mexican version is the chile component. Instead of toasting, hydrating, and blending whole dried chiles, we're starting with good-quality chile powder. Some commercial chile powders are made from bits and pieces of old, sad chiles. The better types are ground from new-crop chiles; this kind of powder is used for convenience, rather than thrift. Some of the chiles from New Mexico and Arizona are also special and worth your attention — and hard to find in any form other than a powder.

I've never seen a powder-based sauce in Mexico; there, chile powder is served as a garnish with pozole — and it's generally the fiery pequín chile, a wild variety from the north that is beloved throughout the country.

Any time you're using powder, triple-check the spelling. Powders marked chili (with an "i" on the end) powder are a blend of spices used for making chili con carne. They can be delicious and handy, or they can be bottom-of-the-barrel bland. For this recipe, you need a powder that's pure chile pepper, so make sure what you use for this recipe is marked chile (with an "e"). When in doubt, check that the ingredients list includes only ground chiles, not other spices.

Making a sauce from chile powder is an American Southwestern tradition. The secret to making a delicious sauce this way is to first fry the chile powder with onions and garlic, then slowly add broth. This type of sauce needs to cook for at least 20 minutes; otherwise, you might end up with a grainy texture.

If you prefer chicken to pork, you could easily substitute it in this recipe.

SOUTHWESTERN RED PORK POSOLE   *serves 8 to 12*

FOR THE MEAT AND BROTH:

2 to 4 pounds bone-in pork shoulder, chopped into large chunks

½ of an onion, chopped

4 garlic cloves, peeled and smashed

1 bay leaf

1 tablespoon salt, or to taste

FOR THE CHILE SAUCE:

¼ cup pure red chile powder

2 cloves

1 teaspoon ground cumin

2 tablespoons oil or lard

¼ of an onion, chopped

3 garlic cloves, peeled and smashed

Salt to taste

TO FINISH:

4 to 6 cups cooked prepared hominy, plus 2 cups of reserved cooking liquid (see page 30)

GARNISHES:

Radishes, sliced thin

Onion, finely chopped

Dried Mexican oregano or Rancho Gordo Oregano Indio

Romaine or iceberg lettuce, sliced very thin

Mexican limes or key limes, quartered

Avocado, cubed

FOR THE MEAT AND BROTH:

In a large stockpot over medium-high heat, add the pork, onion, garlic, bay leaf, salt, and enough water to cover the pork by 1 inch. Bring to a boil, then immediately reduce heat to a gentle simmer, using a lid to help regulate temperature as needed. Continue to simmer until the meat is tender and falling off the bones. Remove the pork pieces to a platter. Once cool enough to handle, separate the meat, discarding bones and skin.

Strain the broth into a very large bowl; cool to room temperature. Chill in the refrigerator for several hours, or overnight, until fat rises to the top of the bowl and congeals. Remove the fat and reserve for another use.

FOR THE CHILE SAUCE:

Using a mortar and pestle, mash the chile powder with the cloves and cumin until smooth. (You can also use a spice grinder for this step.)

In a large pot over medium heat, warm 2 tablespoons of oil or lard. Add the onion and garlic; cook until soft, 5 to 7 minutes. Add the chile powder mixture and stir immediately; a paste will form. Continue cooking for 3 to 4 minutes, stirring constantly. Very slowly, add about a cup of the broth; mix thoroughly. Add another cup of the broth; reduce heat to medium-low and cook another 10 minutes. Taste for salt and adjust seasoning as needed.

TO FINISH:

To the pot with the chile sauce, add the reserved meat, drained hominy, and another cup of pork broth, plus enough extra broth to make a soupy mixture. If you run out of pork broth, use the reserved hominy-cooking liquid. Stir well; raise heat to medium and bring to a simmer. Cook for another 20 to 40 minutes. Taste and adjust seasoning, as desired.

Ladle into bowls and serve with your preferred garnishes.

HOMINY and CHARD in TOMATO SAUCE

This is an original recipe in the manner of New Mexican posole, reinvented as an everyday family meal. While posole is a natural party dish, it's a shame to enjoy it only on special occasions. In his seminal book, *The Feast of Santa Fe*, author Huntley Dent claims that the difference between everyday posole and feast-day posole is the quantity of pork.

This version of the dish happens to be vegetarian, and I think it's terrific on its own and easy enough to throw together at the last minute, especially if you have leftovers like tomato sauce and cooked chard on hand.

Although I'm giving specific ingredients and measurements for this dish, feel free to improvise. You're just smothering cooked hominy in good tomato sauce and then tossing it with cooked chard. If you have spinach on hand, use that. Are you feeling particularly lazy, but want to use up some extra hominy? Use your favorite jarred tomato sauce. My one plea: Please cook the elements separately to keep their flavors distinct.

HOMINY and CHARD in TOMATO SAUCE   *serves 4 to 6*

FOR THE HOMINY:

3 cups cooked prepared hominy, plus 2 cups of
reserved cooking liquid (see page 30)

FOR THE TOMATO SAUCE:

3 thick white or yellow onion slices, skins on

2 garlic cloves, unpeeled

1 stick Rancho Gordo canela (true cinnamon)

3 or 4 whole peeled canned tomatoes, plus
about ¼ cup of their juice

1 teaspoon dried Mexican oregano or
Rancho Gordo Oregano Indio

Chicken or vegetable broth, as needed

2 tablespoons olive oil or lard

Salt, to taste

FOR THE CHARD:

1 bunch green or red chard, leaves separated
from stems

2 tablespoons olive oil

½ of a white onion, chopped

1 jalapeño or serrano chile, minced

FOR THE HOMINY:

In a small pan over medium heat, warm the hominy in its cooking liquid. Reduce heat to low.

FOR THE TOMATO SAUCE:

Warm a dry comal or skillet over medium heat, and roast the onion slices and garlic until soft, about 10 minutes. Remove to a plate. Toast the canela in the same pan, turning often, until it gives off a pleasant aroma, about 2 minutes.

Peel and discard the onion skins and garlic skins. In a blender, combine the peeled onion and garlic, tomatoes, tomato juice, and oregano. Add enough chicken or vegetable broth to allow the blender blades to move, if needed. Blend until smooth.

In a large pan over medium heat, warm the oil or lard. Sauté the tomato mixture with the toasted canela, stirring constantly. Raise heat to medium-high; bring the mixture to a steady simmer. Keep stirring until the mixture tightens to a thick sauce, about 15 minutes. Taste and season with salt; remove the canela. Thin with more broth, as desired.

FOR THE CHARD:

Chop chard stems into small pieces. In a large skillet over medium-high heat, warm the olive oil. Add the chard stems, onion, and chile, cooking until soft, about 10 minutes. Meanwhile, bunch up the chard leaves and slice into ribbons. Add the chard ribbons to the hot pan; stir well so that the hot oil-and-vegetable mixture covers the chard. Reduce heat to medium; add a small amount of the reserved hominy-cooking liquid and simmer until the chard reduces, about 10 minutes, stirring occasionally.

TO FINISH:

For each serving, ladle a portion of hominy into a bowl, cover with the tomato sauce, then toss with the chard. Repeat for each guest.

ACAPULCO-STYLE SEAFOOD POZOLE

Most pozoles made with seafood or fish are white. This version, inspired by Acapulco chef Susana Palazuelos, contains tomatoes, a somewhat unorthodox addition. The best mix of seafood is open to interpretation, but I love the flavor that mussels add. I suggest tossing in the mussels toward the end of cooking, letting them cook in the broth and release their briny liquor into the pot, like a San Francisco–style cioppino or Mediterranean seafood stew. Although this method may not be authentic (I can't imagine any Mexican serving mussels and clams in their shells, making their guests work) it's much less effort for the chef, it looks dramatic, and it's fun for your friends.

ACAPULCO-STYLE SEAFOOD POZOLE
serves 6 to 8

FOR THE CHILE PASTE:

2 ancho chiles, wiped clean with a moist towel

2 guajillo chiles, wiped clean with a moist towel

½ of a head of garlic, broken into cloves

1 cup canned whole peeled Roma tomatoes

1 onion, chopped

TO FINISH:

¼ cup peanut oil

6 to 8 cups fish broth or light chicken broth
(see note, page 41)

3 cups cooked prepared hominy (see page 30)

1 pound firm white fish

1 pound shrimp, peeled and de-veined,
shells reserved if making broth (see note,
page 41)

1 pound mussels in their shells, cleaned
and debearded

1 pound clams, scrubbed

Salt, to taste

GARNISHES:

Onion, chopped

Radishes, thinly sliced

Cilantro, chopped

Mexican limes or key limes, quartered

Dried Mexican oregano or
Rancho Gordo Oregano Indio

FOR THE CHILE PASTE:

Cut the chiles in half; discard seeds and stems. In a small saucepan, warm 2 cups of water over medium-low heat; turn off heat when the water is hot. Meanwhile, warm a dry comal or skillet over medium heat; toast the chiles quickly, taking care not to let them burn. Soak the toasted chiles in the pan of warm water for 15 minutes. Drain chiles, reserving the soaking liquid.

Meanwhile, dry-roast the garlic on the same skillet or comal until soft. Cool, then peel.

In a blender, combine the chiles, garlic, tomatoes, onion, and enough of the strained chile-soaking liquid to allow the blender blades to move. Blend well, scraping down the paste as needed. Use a wooden spoon to push the mixture through a fine-mesh sieve into a small bowl, discarding the skins and seeds.

TO FINISH:

In a large pot over medium heat, warm the oil until hot, 2 to 3 minutes. Add the chile paste and stir immediately. Reduce heat to medium-low; cook, stirring frequently, for 5 to 10 minutes. Add 4 cups of broth; stir well. Add the cooked hominy and heat through. (If you are using canned hominy, rinse the kernels before using and discard the liquid.)

Add the fish and seafood; gently stir to heat through. Add additional broth as needed — the mixture should be very soupy but the ingredients shouldn't feel lost. Taste and add salt, as desired. Cook for another 10 minutes, checking that the fish is cooked through. Discard any unopened clams or mussels.

Ladle into bowls and serve with your preferred garnishes.

PILAR SANCHEZ'S CALIFORNIA POZOLE

Ask longtime Napa Valley residents about Pilar Sanchez and you'll often get a nostalgic sigh. She was on the scene for years but the highlight of her career, for me, was when she and her husband Didier opened Pilar, an intimate, chef-driven restaurant that seemed to be everyone's favorite. In an era where so many restaurants are corporate "concepts" (with corporate investments), it was a pleasure to put yourself in the hands of a true chef and let her do her magic. Pilar served California cuisine but with little touches reminding you of her family's roots in San Luis Potosí.

Pilar's mother was flustered by this nontraditional version of pozole, so Pilar rechristened it California Pozole. It's lighter than the traditional version and makes good use of the abundant zucchini so many of us have during the summer months.

PILAR SANCHEZ'S CALIFORNIA POZOLE

serves 6 to 8

FOR THE CHILE PASTE:

4 guajillo chiles, wiped clean with a moist towel

TO FINISH:

1 tablespoon vegetable oil

1 onion, diced

1 tablespoon minced garlic (from 5 cloves)

8 to 9 cups chicken broth or vegetable broth (preferably homemade)

1 cup celery, diced (from 3 stalks)

1 cup carrots, diced (from 2 medium carrots)

1 cup chayote, peeled and diced (from 1 chayote)

1 cup zucchini, diced (from 1 large zucchini)

4 to 6 cups cooked prepared hominy, plus 2 cups of reserved cooking liquid (see page 30)

1 tablespoon dried Mexican oregano or Rancho Gordo Oregano Indio

Salt, to taste

1 pound shredded cooked chicken meat

GARNISHES:

White cabbage or lettuce, thinly sliced

Radishes, thinly sliced

Avocado, cubed

Mexican limes or key limes, quartered

Cilantro, chopped

Onion, chopped fine

FOR THE CHILE PASTE:

Cut chiles in half; discard seeds and stems. In a small saucepan, warm 2 cups of water over medium-low heat; turn off heat when the water is hot. Meanwhile, warm a dry comal or skillet over medium heat; toast the chiles quickly, taking care not to let the chiles burn. Soak the toasted chiles in the pan of warm water for 15 minutes. Drain chiles, reserving the soaking liquid.

In a blender, combine the chiles and enough of the strained chile-soaking liquid to allow the blender blades to move. Blend well, scraping down the paste as needed. Use a wooden spoon to push the mixture through a fine-mesh sieve into a small bowl, discarding the skins and seeds.

TO FINISH:

In a large stockpot over medium-high heat, warm the oil. Add the onions and stir, allowing them to become translucent without browning. Add the garlic and chile paste; cook, stirring constantly, for 5 minutes. Slowly stir in 8 cups of the broth. Add the celery and carrots; bring the mixture to a boil. Continue cooking until the vegetables just begin to lose their crunch, 10 to 15 minutes.

Add the chayote, zucchini, hominy, and oregano. (If you are using canned hominy, rinse the kernels before using and discard the liquid.) Reduce heat to medium-low; gently simmer until the vegetables are cooked through. Taste and add salt, as desired.

Stir in the chicken meat and gently simmer for another 5 minutes. If the pozole is not soupy enough to your liking, slowly add the reserved hominy-cooking liquid (or tap water, if you used canned hominy) or more broth, until you reach the desired consistency.

Ladle into bowls and serve with your preferred garnishes.

SHRIMP and HOMINY STEW with SMOKED PAPRIKA

I'm not calling this dish pozole because the chile here is the smoked Spanish paprika known as pimentón, and I have a hunch a lot of people would quibble with my vocabulary. So instead, it's a stew! I doubt this kind of thing exists in Spain but it sure was a hit at my house — it will be in heavy rotation for a while.

I think shrimp and celery are a grand combination. Four stalks might sound like a lot, but it cooks down and makes the shrimp very happy.

SHRIMP and HOMINY STEW with SMOKED PAPRIKA

serves 6 to 8

FOR THE BASE:

3 tablespoons olive oil

4 stalks celery, sliced thin

1 yellow onion, diced

3 garlic cloves, minced

1 teaspoon dried Mexican oregano or Rancho Gordo Oregano Indio

3 tablespoons smoked Spanish paprika

1 teaspoon dried thyme

TO FINISH:

4 to 5 cups liquid (hominy-cooking liquid, bean broth, meat or seafood broth, or any combination)

3 cups cooked prepared hominy (see page 30)

1 pound raw shrimp, peeled and de-veined, shells reserved if making broth (see note, page 41)

GARNISHES:

Fresh parsley, chopped

1 lemon, quartered

FOR THE BASE:

In a stockpot over medium heat, warm the olive oil. Add the celery, onion, and garlic; cook until soft, 10 to 15 minutes. Add oregano, paprika, and thyme. Continue cooking for a few minutes, stirring until a thick paste forms.

TO FINISH:

Slowly add 4 cups of liquid, stirring constantly until warmed, about 5 minutes. Add the hominy. Once the soup is warm, add the shrimp and simmer until just cooked, about 5 minutes. Add the last cup of liquid if the stew seems too thick for your taste.

Ladle into bowls and allow guests to add parsley and a squeeze of lemon, as desired.

GREEN

CLASSIC GUERRERO GREEN POZOLE

In the state of Guerrero, Thursday is considered pozole day, much like
Monday is the traditional time for red beans and rice in Louisiana. I was in
Taxco with some friends a few years ago, and it wasn't easy to get a good
restaurant meal in that otherwise lovely town. We passed a *pozolería* several times but, frustratingly, it always seemed to be closed. On Thursday, we
walked by and the place was finally open — we had our best meal of the trip.

The most famous pozole from Guerrero is pozole verde, and with good
reason. It's rich, complicated, and yet not too difficult to prepare. It's somewhat exotic and familiar at the same time. The addition of pumpkin seeds
(known in Mexico as pepitas) isn't exclusive to pozole verde, but this dish
tastes much different than a classic *pipián* sauce, which has a base of
pumpkin seeds.

CLASSIC GUERRERO GREEN POZOLE   *serves 8 to 12*

FOR THE MEAT AND BROTH:

2 to 4 pounds bone-in pork shoulder, chopped into large chunks

1 pound bone-in country-style pork ribs

1 pig trotter (optional), chopped into 6 pieces

½ of an onion, sliced

3 garlic cloves, peeled and smashed

2 bay leaves

3 cloves, roughly smashed

3 black peppercorns, roughly cracked

1 tablespoon salt, or to taste

FOR THE TOMATILLO PASTE:

1 pound tomatillos, papery husks removed, rinsed and halved

2 to 4 serrano chiles, stems removed

3 garlic cloves, peeled

3 epazote sprigs

1 bunch radish greens

½ cup cilantro

1 teaspoon ground cumin

Salt, to taste

2 cups roasted hulled pumpkin seeds (pepitas), ground

TO FINISH:

4 to 6 cups cooked prepared hominy, plus 2 cups of reserved cooking liquid (see page 30)

GARNISHES:

Radishes, sliced thin

Onion, finely chopped

Chile de Árbol Salsa (see page 56)

Dried Mexican oregano or
Rancho Gordo Oregano Indio

Romaine or iceberg lettuce, sliced very thin

Mexican limes or key limes, quartered

Avocado, cubed

Chicharrón

FOR THE MEAT AND BROTH:

In a large stockpot over medium-high heat, add the pork shoulder, ribs, trotter (if using), onion, garlic, bay leaves, cloves, peppercorns, salt, and enough
water to cover meat by 1 inch. Bring to a boil, then immediately reduce heat to a gentle simmer, using a lid to help regulate temperature as needed. Skim and discard any impurities that rise to the top. Continue to simmer for several hours until meat is tender and falling off the bones.

Remove the pork pieces to a platter. Strain the broth into a very large bowl; cool to room temperature. Chill in the refrigerator for several hours, or overnight, until fat rises to the top of the bowl and congeals. Remove the fat and reserve for another use.

FOR THE TOMATILLO PASTE:

In a blender, combine the tomatillos, chiles, garlic, epazote, radish greens, cilantro, cumin, salt, and enough liquid to allow the blender blades to move. Pulse, scraping down the blender as needed, until mixture is coarse and relish-like.

In a large pot over medium-low heat, warm the tomatillo paste; cook, stirring frequently, for about 10 minutes. Stir in the ground pumpkin seeds and cook, stirring, for another 10 minutes. Taste and adjust seasoning, as desired.

TO FINISH:

To the pot with the tomatillo paste, add the reserved pork meat and the drained cooked hominy. (If you are using canned hominy, rinse the kernels before using and discard the liquid.) You can break up large pieces of meat as needed, but generally they'll do this on their own.

Slowly add about 6 cups of the broth, enough to make a soupy stew, stirring constantly. If the pozole is not soupy enough to your liking, slowly add the reserved hominy-cooking liquid (or tap water, if you used canned hominy) or more broth, until you reach the desired consistency.

Continue cooking, stirring occasionally, until all of the ingredients are warmed through, about 20 minutes (or longer if you've pulled your pork and corn from the refrigerator).

Ladle into bowls and serve with your preferred garnishes.

VARIATIONS

Many recipes feature a seeded, roasted, peeled poblano chile in the mix. I don't think it adds much (except more work). Others will vehemently disagree.

Diana Kennedy and other cooks use sorrel leaves. There's a wild sorrel called axoxoco *in Guerrero — good luck finding that! If I find sorrel in the market or while I'm foraging, I'll be making her version; until then, the sour flavor will have to come from the tomatillos.*

Susana Palazuelos is a renowned chef in Acapulco with some great books to her name — Mexico, una Herencia de Sabores being my favorite. Her pozole verde uses pork trotters and chicken, plus peanuts as a thickener

ALTA BAJA'S VEGAN POZOLE VERDE

Delilah Snell runs a great store and eatery in the heart of Santa Ana, California, called Alta Baja. On one visit, Delilah slipped me a bowl of her pozole verde. It's an untraditional version but, at the same time, it will be familiar to anyone who loves pozole.

Delilah's recipe was developed with the help of a staff member, Juana, who hails from Guerrero. The recipe uses parsley as a substitute for hoja santa, and omits the usual epazote. Feel free to add one or both along with the parsley, if you have access to them.

I hope you are lucky enough to enjoy the pozole at Alta Baja one day. If not, Delilah's famous dish — which has also been featured in *The New Yorker* — is yours to make.

ALTA BAJA'S VEGAN POZOLE VERDE *serves 6*

FOR THE CHILE PASTE:

5 dried pasilla chiles, wiped clean with
a moist towel

1 large onion

2 green bell peppers

4 garlic cloves

3 large tomatillos

2 jalapeño chiles

1 serrano chile

3 Anaheim, Hungarian, banana, or Italian peppers

1 cup roasted hulled pumpkin seeds (pepitas)

1 bunch parsley, coarsely chopped

1 teaspoon salt, or to taste

TO FINISH:

6 cups cooked prepared hominy (see page 30)

1½ cups cooked pinto or black beans, drained

1 zucchini or other summer squash, cut into
bite-size cubes

GARNISHES:

Extra-virgin olive oil

2 avocados, sliced

1 cup finely shredded red cabbage

½ cup sliced serrano peppers

½ cup finely diced red onion

¼ cup dried Mexican oregano or
Rancho Gordo Oregano Indio

3 Mexican limes or key limes, quartered

4 radishes, thinly sliced or julienned

Tostadas or tortilla chips, for dunking

FOR THE CHILE PASTE:

Heat the oven to 375°F.

In a small saucepan, warm 2 cups of water over medium-low heat; turn off heat when the water is hot. Soak the pasilla chiles in the pan of warm water for 5 minutes. Drain chiles, reserving the soaking liquid.

Halve the onion and bell peppers. Place on sheet pan with unpeeled garlic, unhusked tomatillos, and all of the fresh chiles and peppers. Roast in the preheated oven until soft and beginning to brown, about 30 minutes. Remove from the oven; let cool for 10 minutes.

Stem and seed the roasted peppers and all the chiles; remove tomatillo husks, and peel the garlic and onion.

In a blender, combine the pasilla chiles, roasted vegetables, pumpkin seeds, parsley, and enough of the strained chile-soaking liquid to allow the blender blades to move. Pulse, scraping down the blender as needed, until the mixture is coarse and relish-like.

In a medium pot over medium heat, combine the chile mixture with enough water to achieve a stew-like consistency. Season with salt. Bring to a boil, then reduce heat to low; simmer for 10 minutes.

TO FINISH:

Add the hominy and beans; simmer for 5 minutes. Add the squash; simmer for 1 to 2 minutes, until the mixture is heated through but the squash maintains some crunch.

Ladle into bowls; top with a generous drizzle of olive oil and slices of avocado. Serve with your preferred garnishes, and tostadas or tortilla chips on the side.

NEW MEXICAN POSOLE VERDE

In New Mexico, eating hominy seems to be a more casual affair than in Mexico. Posole — both the grain and the dish — doesn't require a gathering to be served. It's not unusual to have a simple bowl of posole as a side dish. If you're ordering sopapillas or enchiladas, adding pozole to your meal may seem like a lot of starch, but I find it impossible to say no.

A southwestern green posole gets its color from fresh chiles, not the herbs and greens you'd find in a Guerrero-style pozole. I was initially partial to the more exotic Mexican green pozole but this New Mexico dish is great in its own right, and deserves to be a part of your repertoire. Like chili con carne, I find it nostalgic, even though it has nothing to do with my own past. Chiles from Hatch, New Mexico, are rightly famous — if you have them, use them. Anaheim and even poblano chiles make fine substitutes. You could use good canned chiles but roasting them yourself isn't so difficult and they have a superior taste.

Southwestern garnishes for posole don't tend to be as elaborate as those in Mexico, but a little chopped onion and lime is always appreciated. I've heard of grated cheese as a garnish, too, but I'm going to pretend that i haven't.

NEW MEXICAN POSOLE VERDE   *serves 6 to 8*

FOR THE MEAT AND BROTH:

2 to 3 pounds bone-in country-style pork ribs

½ of an onion, chopped

3 garlic cloves, smashed

1 bay leaf

1 tablespoon salt, or to taste

FOR THE CHILES:

4 to 5 Anaheim chiles (or poblanos or
New Mexican chiles), about 1 pound

2 serrano chiles, finely chopped

TO FINISH:

2 tablespoons olive oil

1 onion, chopped

4 to 5 garlic cloves, minced

1 teaspoon ground cumin

1 teaspoon ground clove

1 tablespoon New Mexican chile powder

2 to 3 cups cooked prepared hominy, plus 2 cups
of reserved cooking liquid (see page 30)

GARNISHES:

Radishes, sliced thin

Onion, finely chopped

New Mexican chile powder

Dried Mexican oregano or
Rancho Gordo Oregano Indio

Crisp lettuce or cabbage, sliced very thin

Mexican limes or key limes, quartered

Cilantro, chopped

FOR THE MEAT AND BROTH:

In a large stockpot over medium-high heat, add the ribs, onion, garlic, bay leaf, salt, and enough water to cover meat by 1 inch. Bring to a boil, then immediately reduce heat to a gentle simmer, using a lid to help regulate temperature as needed. Skim and discard any impurities that rise to the top. Continue to simmer for about 90 minutes, adding hot water as needed to keep the meat covered, until meat is tender and falling off the bones.

Remove the pork pieces to a platter. Once cool enough to handle, separate the meat, discarding the bones.

Strain the broth into a very large bowl; cool to room temperature. Chill in the refrigerator for several hours, or overnight, until fat rises to the top of the bowl and congeals. Remove the fat and reserve for another use.

FOR THE CHILES:

Roast the Anaheim chiles over a gas burner, rotating frequently until all sides are well charred. (Alternatively, you can heat a dry comal or skillet over high heat and char the chiles by rolling them around the hot pan.) Place the charred chiles in a large bowl; cover with a plate and rest for about 30 minutes. Remove and discard the charred skin. Halve the chiles and remove seeds; wipe the chiles to remove stray bits of burned skin, but try to save any juices. Roughly chop the cleaned chiles and combine with the chopped serrano chiles.

TO FINISH:

In a large pot over medium heat, warm the oil. Add the onion and garlic; cook until soft, about 7 minutes. Add the cumin, clove, and chile powder; mix well. Add the chiles, the cooked hominy, and the reserved meat. Mix well.

Add the broth slowly, enough to make a soupy mixture but not so much that the corn and meat are floating, about 7 cups. If you need more liquid, add the reserved hominy-cooking liquid, more broth, or water. Taste and adjust seasoning, as desired. Partially cover the pan and cook for about an hour, reducing heat as needed to maintain a gentle simmer.

Ladle into bowls and serve with your preferred garnishes.

MUSHROOM POZOLE

This is a delicious twist on pozole but you really need a great stock. If you're not concerned about keeping this dish vegetarian, I'd use chicken stock, but vegetable stock can be delicious, especially if you make it yourself.

I made a big batch of this recipe and brought some of the leftovers to a friend. She said she liked it. She later called back and said she loved it because she used the limes I'd sent over for a second bowl. Limes can make a good dish great.

The color isn't as glorious as the flavor, so make sure you have lots of cilantro on hand to brighten the dish.

MUSHROOM POZOLE

serves 6 to 8

FOR THE TOMATILLO PASTE:

1 large white or yellow onion, cut into 3 large slices, skins removed

4 garlic cloves

½ pound tomatillos, papery husks removed

¼ cup roasted hulled pumpkin seeds (pepitas)

6 cloves, crushed

3 jalapeños en escabeche, drained and roughly chopped

1 tablespoon dried Mexican oregano or Rancho Gordo Oregano Indio

2 tablespoons olive oil

TO FINISH:

1½ pounds button mushrooms, thickly sliced

3 tablespoons olive oil

Salt, to taste

2 large sticks Rancho Gordo canela (true cinnamon)

4 to 6 cups cooked prepared hominy, plus 2 cups of reserved cooking liquid (see page 30)

1 quart chicken broth or vegetable broth

GARNISHES:

Fresh cilantro, chopped

Roasted hulled pumpkin seeds (pepitas)

Mexican or key limes, halved

FOR THE TOMATILLO PASTE:

Warm a dry comal or skillet over medium-high heat. Roast the onion slices and unpeeled garlic, turning occasionally, until charred and slightly softened, 15 to 20 minutes. Transfer to a bowl and let rest.

Add the tomatillos to the skillet; roast until soft and starting to hiss. Roll tomatillos around, doing your best to get the skins evenly roasted. Add the tomatillos to the resting vegetables. When cool, peel the garlic and discard skins.

In a blender, combine the roasted vegetables, pumpkin seeds, cloves, jalapeños, and oregano; blend well. Add just enough of the hominy-cooking liquid to move the blades.

In a large stockpot over medium-high heat, warm 2 tablespoons of olive oil. Add the vegetable puree; adjust heat to maintain a simmer. Cook, stirring occasionally, for 10 minutes.

TO FINISH:

Meanwhile, in a bowl, toss mushrooms with 3 tablespoons olive oil and a good pinch of salt. Heat a large skillet over medium-high heat until just smoking. Add mushroom mixture and the canela; cook for 5 minutes, until mushrooms start to release their juices.

Add the mushrooms and the canela to the vegetable mixture, along with the cooked hominy. Stir well; add enough hominy-cooking liquid or broth to make a thick soupy mixture. Taste and adjust seasoning, as desired. Reduce heat to medium. Gently simmer for 20 minutes, allowing the starches from the corn to thicken the soup.

If the pozole is not soupy enough to your liking, add more broth. Taste again and adjust seasoning, adding more salt or chopped jalapeños to taste. Remove the canela.

Ladle into bowls, top with cilantro and a few pepitas, and serve with limes.

GREEN POZOLE with SHRIMP

As much as I love pork and chicken, some of my happiest memories have been made over a bucket of perfect shrimp. Any type of pozole is appropriate for any time of year, but I think a party with shrimp pozole, cold beers, and a fun crowd sounds like summer.

I think it's better to buy the much more expensive wild-caught shrimp. There are a lot of reasons, moral and culinary, not to buy farmed shrimp. (I'll let you look them up yourself instead of sharing them here.)

GREEN POZOLE with SHRIMP   *serves 6 to 8*

FOR THE TOMATILLO PASTE:

½ pound tomatillos, papery husks removed, rinsed and halved

3 garlic cloves, peeled and smashed

1 cup cilantro, chopped

2 serrano or jalapeño chiles, stemmed and roughly chopped

TO FINISH:

3 cups cooked prepared hominy (see page 30)

8 cups fish or chicken broth, or a broth made from shrimp shells (see note, page 41)

Salt

2 tablespoons olive oil

¼ cup finely chopped onion

2½ to 3 pounds wild-caught shrimp, peeled and de-veined, shells reserved if making broth (see note, page 41)

1 cup roasted hulled pumpkin seeds (pepitas), ground

2 teaspoons dried shrimp powder (optional)

GARNISHES:

Lettuce, sliced very thin

Red onion, finely chopped

Dried Mexican oregano or Rancho Gordo Oregano Indio

Radishes, sliced thin

Mexican limes or key limes, quartered

Tostadas

FOR THE TOMATILLO PASTE:

In a blender, combine the tomatillos, garlic, cilantro, chiles, and enough liquid to allow the blender blades to move. Blend well, scraping down the blender as needed.

TO FINISH:

In a large pot over medium heat, warm the cooked hominy in the broth. Reduce heat to low, maintaining a gentle simmer. Add salt to taste.

In another pot over medium heat, warm the olive oil. Add the onions; cook, stirring occasionally, until softened, about 5 minutes. Add the shrimp, stirring until cooked through, about 3 minutes; remove to a platter.

Add the tomatillo paste to the pan, stirring to scrape up any clinging bits of shrimp. Cook for 5 minutes; add the ground pumpkin seeds and shrimp powder, if using, and continue to cook until thickened, about 3 minutes.

Add the tomatillo mixture and shrimp to the hominy-broth mixture; gently cook until warm, 2 to 3 minutes.

Ladle into bowls and serve with your preferred garnishes.

RANCHO GORDO GREEN POSOLE

This is an early version of a southwestern-style posole. The base is mostly tomatillos (or *tomate verde*, as they're known in most of Mexico). If you're a home gardener, you'll enjoy how easy they are to grow. There are several varieties, my favorite being the small, purple-ish *milperos*. Fair warning: Once you grow them, you're likely to have them come back year after year. Each fruit has lots of seeds, and even with diligent harvesting, you're bound to have this welcome guest return to your garden each spring.

When you peel the husks, save them for cooking nopales (cactus paddles). Placing several husks in a pot with the paddles helps to absorb some of the gooey liquid that they exude.

RANCHO GORDO GREEN POSOLE   *serves 6*

FOR THE CHILE SAUCE:

1½ onions, white or red, peeled and halved

4 garlic cloves, peeled

15 to 20 tomatillos, papery husks removed

2 poblano chiles

1 serrano chile

2 tablespoons extra virgin olive oil

½ cup roasted hulled pumpkin seeds (pepitas), ground

1 cup coarsely chopped cilantro

2 teaspoons dried Mexican oregano or Rancho Gordo Oregano Indio

5 to 6 cups vegetable broth or chicken broth

TO FINISH:

2 cups button mushrooms, sliced

2 fresh epazote sprigs (optional)

2 tablespoons olive oil

Salt and freshly ground black pepper

2 cups cooked prepared hominy, plus 2 cups of reserved cooking liquid (see page 30)

GARNISHES:

Lettuce, sliced very thin

Red onion, finely chopped

Dried Mexican oregano or Rancho Gordo Oregano Indio

Radishes, sliced thin

Mexican limes or key limes, quartered

Tostadas

FOR THE CHILE SAUCE:

Warm a dry comal or skillet over medium heat. Roast the onions, garlic, tomatillos, and chiles, turning occasionally, until charred and slightly softened, 15 to 20 minutes. Work in batches, if necessary.

Stem the serrano chile, but don't skin or seed it. Place the poblano chiles in a large bowl; cover with a plate and rest for about 30 minutes. Transfer the other vegetables to a bowl and let cool, collecting their juices. Remove chiles from the bowl; remove and discard the charred skin. Halve each chile, removing stems, ribs, and seeds.

In a blender, working in batches if necessary, combine the roasted chiles, vegetables and their juices, and enough of the hominy-cooking liquid to allow the blender blades to move. Blend well, scraping down blender as needed.

In a large stockpot over medium heat, warm the oil. Add the vegetable puree; adjust heat to maintain a simmer. Cook, stirring occasionally, for 10 minutes. Stir in the ground pumpkin seeds and cook, stirring, for another 10 minutes.

In the blender, combine the cilantro, oregano, and 1 cup of broth; blend well. Add to the vegetable mixture along with 4 additional cups of broth.

TO FINISH:

In a medium bowl, toss the mushrooms with the epazote (if using), olive oil, and a bit of salt. In a medium skillet over high heat, cook the mushroom mixture until just browned, about 5 minutes, stirring occasionally. Reduce heat to medium; cook for another 5 minutes, until mushrooms are tender.

Add the hominy to the vegetable-puree pot. Cook until warm, 10 to 15 minutes. Add the mushroom mixture and adjust seasoning, then return to a simmer. Thin with additional broth, if necessary.

Ladle into bowls and serve with your preferred garnishes.

POZOLE de la INDEPENDENCIA

I've adapted this recipe from the book *Guanajuato: Sabor y Historia*, but I haven't been able to find any other reference to this dish, even from friends in Guanajuato. I suspect it's an original creation or family recipe making the best use of local ingredients. I like it because it incorporates the sour prickly pears known as *xoconostle*. I haven't seen them used in pozole before and I love the idea, especially since this region produces so many varieties of *xoconostle*.

POZOLE de la INDEPENDENCIA   *serves 8 to 12*

FOR THE MEAT AND BROTH:

6 whole chicken wings

3 bone-in chicken breasts

2 onions, chopped

2 heads of garlic

1 tablespoon salt, or to taste

FOR THE SALSA VERDE:

20 pieces dried plain *xoconostle*

2 pounds tomatillos, papery husks removed, rinsed and halved

1½ cups cilantro

3 garlic cloves, peeled and smashed

¼ cup chopped onion

2 serrano chiles, stems removed

2 epazote sprigs

2 tablespoons corn oil

Salt, to taste

TO FINISH:

4 to 6 cups cooked prepared hominy, plus 2 cups of reserved cooking liquid (see page 30)

GARNISHES:

Romaine lettuce, sliced very thin

Radishes, sliced thin

Onion, chopped

Pequín chile, crumbled or powder

Dried Mexican oregano or Rancho Gordo Oregano Indio

Tostadas

Mexican limes or key limes, quartered

FOR THE CHICKEN AND BROTH
(BEST DONE A DAY AHEAD):

In a large stockpot over high heat, combine the chicken wings and breasts with the onion, garlic, salt and 8 cups of water. Bring to a boil, then immediately reduce heat to a gentle simmer, using a lid to help regulate temperature as needed. Cook for about an hour, removing the chicken breasts to a platter after 25 to 30 minutes so they don't overcook.

Remove pan from heat. Remove the chicken wings to the platter. Once cool enough to handle, separate the meat, discarding bones and skin. Reserve the breast and wing meat.

Strain the broth into a very large bowl; cool to room temperature. Chill in the refrigerator for several hours, or overnight, until fat rises to the top of the bowl and congeals. Remove the fat and reserve for another use.

FOR THE SALSA VERDE:

Soak the *xoconostle* in warm water for 2 hours. When soft, drain well, reserving the soaking liquid.

In a blender, working in batches if needed, combine the *xoconostle*, tomatillos, cilantro, garlic, onion, chiles, epazote, and enough of the hominy-cooking liquid to allow the blender blades to move. Blend well, scraping down the sauce as needed.

In a large pot over medium heat, warm the oil until hot, 2 to 3 minutes. Add the salsa verde and stir immediately. Reduce heat to medium-low; cook, stirring frequently, for 5 to 10 minutes. Taste and adjust seasoning, as desired.

TO FINISH:

To the pot with the salsa verde, add the reserved chicken meat and the drained cooked hominy. (If you are using canned hominy, rinse the kernels before using and discard the liquid.)

Slowly add about 6 cups of broth, enough to make a soupy stew, stirring constantly. If the pozole is not soupy enough to your liking, slowly add the reserved hominy-cooking liquid (or tap water, if you used canned hominy) or more broth, until you reach the desired consistency. You can also add some of the reserved *xoconostle* soaking liquid, if you like.

Continue cooking over medium heat, stirring occasionally, until all of the ingredients are warmed through, about 20 minutes (or a bit longer if you've pulled your chicken and corn from the refrigerator).

Ladle into bowls and serve with your preferred garnishes.

WHITE

MEXICO CITY–SYLE WHITE POZOLE

Many people ask me for restaurant recommendations for Mexico City but I normally have nothing unusual to offer. I haven't spent time there in many years. I land at the airport and, more often than not, I'm greeted by my friends Yunuen Quiroz and Gabriel Garcia. They whisk me off to Pozolería Blanquita for a meal before we hit the road to Hidalgo, Oaxaca, or Puebla.

Pozolería Blanquita is known for its pozole blanco with its rich broth. It's here that I learned to love habanero chile relish — now I use it to garnish quesadillas and bowls of beans, and as a base for other salsas.

MEXICO CITY–STYLE WHITE POZOLE

serves 8 to 10

FOR THE MEAT AND BROTH:

2 to 4 pounds bone-in pork shoulder, chopped into large chunks

1 pound bone-in country-style pork ribs

1 pig trotter (optional), chopped into 6 pieces

½ of an onion, sliced

3 garlic cloves, peeled and smashed

2 bay leaves

3 black peppercorns, roughly cracked

1 tablespoon salt, or to taste

FOR THE CHILE RELISH:

4 to 5 habanero chiles or manzano chiles, stemmed and sliced very thin

½ of a white or red onion, peeled and sliced very thin

1 teaspoon dried Mexican oregano or Rancho Gordo Oregano Indio

¼ cup mild white vinegar or pineapple vinegar, or lime juice

Salt, to taste

TO FINISH:

4 to 6 cups cooked prepared hominy, plus 2 cups of reserved cooking liquid (see page 30)

GARNISHES:

Radishes, sliced thin

Onion, finely chopped

Dried Mexican oregano or Rancho Gordo Oregano Indio

Romaine or iceberg lettuce, sliced very thin

Mexican limes or key limes, quartered

Pequín chile powder

Avocado, cubed

Chicharrón (see variation, page 125)

FOR THE MEAT AND BROTH:

In a large stockpot over medium-high heat, add the pork shoulder, ribs, trotter (if using), onion, garlic, bay leaves, peppercorns, salt, and enough water to cover meat by 1 inch. Bring to a boil, then immediately reduce heat to a gentle simmer, using a lid to help regulate temperature as needed. Skim and discard any impurities that rise to the top. Continue to simmer for several hours, adding hot water as needed to keep the meat covered, until meat is tender and falling off the bones.

Remove the pork pieces to a platter. Once cool enough to handle, separate the meat, discarding bones and skin.

Strain the broth into a very large bowl; cool to room temperature. Chill in the refrigerator for several hours, or overnight, until fat rises to the top of the bowl and congeals. Remove the fat and reserve for another use.

FOR THE CHILE RELISH:

In a small bowl, toss all the ingredients; allow to rest for at least 30 minutes before serving.

TO FINISH:

In a stockpot over medium heat, combine the hominy, meat, and enough of the broth to make a soupy stew. (If you are using canned hominy, rinse the kernels before using and discard the liquid.) Cook until warm, 10 to 15 minutes. Add more broth as needed, or some of the reserved hominy-cooking liquid if you run out of broth.

Ladle into bowls and serve with the fresh chile relish and your other preferred garnishes.

VARIATION

While Guerrero is most famously known for its green pozole, they also have a white version, similar to this, but with pieces of chicharrón on the table for garnish. The chicharrónes make a snap-crackle-pop sound as they hydrate in the pozole liquid and they're incredibly delicious.

OAXACAN POZOLE MIXTECO

So many regions of Mexico have their own twist on pozole and, of course, Oaxaca is no different. This variation comes from the state's La Mixteca region and although this recipe calls for pork, chicken is more common in the area.

The addition of hoja santa (*Piper auritum*) is essential. This herb — also known as *hierba santa*, *yerba santa*, and, in Veracruz, *acuyo* — has a gentle anise flavor that gets mellower as the hominy cooks.

In Oaxaca, mole colorado — a rich seasoning paste that's starkly different from the more widely known mole poblano, from the neighboring state of Puebla — is a common addition, replacing the familiar chile de árbol salsa. Alas, the recipe for mole is beyond the scope of this book. But I bet you can imagine how delicious that would be. If you don't make your own mole colorado, please use one of the Chile de Árbol Salsa recipes on pages 56 and 57. It's better to use a great salsa than a bad mole.

This pozole, using corn cooked with hoja santa leaves, is also commonly cooked with chicken. Many indigenous communities prefer chicken and find it more digestible.

OAXACAN POZOLE MIXTECO

serves 8 to 12

FOR THE POSOLE:

½ pound Rancho Gordo Prepared
Hominy/White Corn Posole, uncooked

3 hoja santa leaves (see note, page 127)

½ of an onion, chopped

FOR THE MEAT AND BROTH:

2 to 3 pounds bone-in pork shoulder

1 pig trotter, chopped into 6 pieces

1 onion, peeled and halved

2 garlic cloves, peeled and smashed

2 cloves

1 bay leaf

1 tablespoon salt, or to taste

GARNISHES:

Chile de Árbol Salsa (see page 56)

Radishes, sliced thin

Onion, finely chopped

Dried Mexican oregano or Rancho Gordo
Oregano Indio

Romaine or iceberg lettuce, sliced very thin

Mexican limes or key limes, quartered

Pequín chile powder

Avocado, cubed

FOR THE POSOLE:

In a large bowl, soak prepared hominy in enough water to cover by 2 inches; let sit 5 to 8 hours.

In a large stockpot over high heat, combine the prepared hominy and its soaking water. Add additional water, if needed, to cover the hominy by about 2 inches. Add the hoja santa and onion; bring to a boil. Cook for 10 minutes, then reduce heat to medium-low. Continue cooking at a gentle simmer until the prepared hominy is tender, about 90 minutes. Partially cover the pot as needed to regulate heat, but don't cover completely or hominy may turn gummy.

Check occasionally, adding hot water, as needed, to keep the corn covered by about an inch. The hominy is done when it's no longer chalky but retains some texture. The kernel will also pop at one end, causing the hominy to blossom. (Because life is unfair, once in awhile you will get a batch that won't flower.)

Strain the hominy, reserving at least 2 cups of the cooking liquid for use in your pozole. Discard the hoja santa.

FOR THE MEAT AND BROTH:

In a large stockpot over medium-high heat, add the pork shoulder, trotter, onion, garlic, cloves, bay leaf, salt, and enough water to cover meat by 1 inch. Bring to a boil, then immediately reduce heat to a gentle simmer, using a lid to help regulate temperature as needed. Skim and discard any impurities that rise to the top. Continue to simmer for several hours, adding hot water as needed to keep the meat covered, until meat is tender and falling off the bones.

Remove the pork pieces to a platter. Once cool enough to handle, separate the meat, discarding bones and skin.

Strain the broth into a very large bowl; cool to room temperature. Chill in the refrigerator for several hours, or overnight, until fat rises to the top of the bowl and congeals. Remove the fat and reserve for another use.

TO FINISH:

In a stockpot over medium heat, combine the hominy, meat, and enough of the broth to make a soupy stew. Cook until thoroughly warm, 10 to 15 minutes. Taste and adjust seasoning. Add more broth as needed, or some of the reserved hominy-cooking liquid, if you run out of broth.

Ladle into bowls and serve with your preferred garnishes.

SHRIMP POZOLE

Jalisco has its own version of shrimp pozole. Frozen, peeled shrimp are handy, but if you do this the slow, laborious way you'll have a better final product. Once you've done a few chores — making the broth and the salsa — the rest comes together quickly. But you can cheat and buy some fish broth, or even use chicken broth, if you must.

SHRIMP POZOLE

serves 8 to 10

FOR THE SHRIMP AND BROTH:

3 to 3½ pounds shell-on shrimp

1 head of garlic, broken into cloves and peeled

2 medium onions, peeled and halved

1 stalk celery

1 bay leaf

FOR THE SALSA:

10 ancho chiles, wiped clean with a moist towel

1 to 2 chiles de árbol, wiped clean with a moist towel

1 garlic clove, peeled and smashed

½ of an onion, chopped

½ cup white vinegar

TO FINISH:

4 to 6 cups cooked prepared hominy (see page 30)

GARNISHES:

Chopped lettuce

Mexican limes or key limes, quartered

Chopped onion

Dried Mexican oregano or Rancho Gordo Oregano Indio

Tostadas

Chile Relish (see page 124)

FOR THE SHRIMP AND BROTH:

Peel and de-vein the shrimp, reserving the shells; refrigerate the shrimp until ready to use. In a stockpot over medium heat, combine the shrimp shells and 8 cups of water; cook for 25 minutes. Strain the broth into a large bowl; discard the shells and return the strained broth to the pot. Add the garlic, onion, celery, and bay leaf. Simmer for 40 minutes over medium heat, uncovered. Strain the broth again into the bowl and then return to the pot; discard the solids.

FOR THE SALSA:

Cut the chiles in half; discard seeds and stems. Warm a dry comal or skillet over medium heat; toast the chiles quickly, taking care not to let the chiles burn. In a medium bowl, combine the toasted chiles with enough of the warm shrimp broth to cover chiles by 1 inch; soak for 15 minutes.

Strain the broth and return it to the pot. In a blender, combine the chiles, garlic, onion, and vinegar. Blend well, scraping down the blender as needed.

TO FINISH THE POZOLE:

Add the hominy to the simmering shrimp broth; cook for 10 minutes. Taste and adjust seasoning, as desired, then add the reserved shrimp; cook, stirring, until cooked through, about 5 minutes. Stir in the salsa.

Ladle into bowls and serve with your preferred garnishes.

BIBLIOGRAPHY

Cocina Regional, Filiberto Enriquez Perales, La Cuija Zacatecas, 1999

Coyote Cafe: Recipes from Santa Fe, Mark Miller, Ten Speed Press, 1989

Frida's Fiestas: Recipes and Reminiscences of Life with Frida Kahlo, Guadalupe Rivera
and Marie-Pierre Colle, Clarkson Potter, 1994

Guanajuato: Sabor e Historia, Monica Solis Vieyra and Maria Loson de Fabregas, Grupo Emyco, 2003

In the Charcuterie, Toponia Miller and Taylor Boetticher, Ten Speed Press, 2013

La Sazón de la Cocina Afromestiza de Guerrero — Cocina Indigena y Popular No. 56, Francisca Aparicio
Prudente, Consejo Nacional para la Cultura y las Artes, 2007

Mexico, una Herencia de Sabores, Susana Palazuelos, Grijalbo, 2010

Nopalito: A Mexican Kitchen, Gonzalo Guzmán, Ten Speed Press, 2017

Pozoles: Sabor y Tradicion, Cocina Practica Mexicana, 2011

Sopas, Patricia Quintana, Océano, 2007

The Essential Cuisines of Mexico, Diana Kennedy, Clarkson Potter 2000

The Feast of Santa Fe: Cooking of the American Southwest, Huntley Dent, Simon & Schuster, 1985

Un Mar de Sabor, Guadalupe Garcia de León del Paso and Leticia Alexander, Índice Editores, 2012

INDEX

A book is always a cooperative effort and this one is no exception. I'd like to thank Julia Newberry for being the heart and soul of this company and the brains behind this project. I'd like to thank Meghan Hildebrand for her inspired design and patience. Special thanks to James Schrupp and Justin Lucero for always making sure we have posole and hominy available.

Special thanks to Deborah Madison for introducing me to Ray Redcorn and the world of southwestern posole.

Thanks to Anita Epler Crotty for her much-appreciated knowledge of Mexican food and the English language. Her editing made this a stronger book.

Extra special thanks to my guinea pigs and researchers: Mary Lee Sando, Nico Sando, Gabriel Cortes, Yunuen Carillo Quiroz, Marge Caldwell, Carl Bunch, Christopher Ann Cowan, Janet Holmberg, Oscar Aguilar Olea, Azalea Aguilar, Nuria Teruel, and Fernando Ventosa.